Goliat

Goliat

Rhiannon Hooson

Seren is the book imprint of
Poetry Wales Press Ltd.
Suite 6, 4 Derwen Road, Bridgend, Wales, CF31 1LH
www.serenbooks.com
facebook.com/SerenBooks
twitter@SerenBooks

The right of Rhiannon Hooson to be identified as
the author of this work has been asserted in accordance
with the Copyright, Designs and Patents Act, 1988.

ISBN: 978-1-78172-656-3
Ebook: 978-1-7817-657-0

A CIP record for this title is available from the British Library.

The publisher acknowledges the financial assistance of the Books Council of Wales.

Cover artwork: 'Half Light' by Jenna Barton

Printed in Bembo by Pulsioprint, France

Contents

All ghosts wear clothes of this colour

A note found in Frida Kahlo's sketchbook read: "greenish yellow: All ghosts wear clothes of this colour."

I loved you only in the garden
women go to when they sleep.

I loved you in clearings where leaves
were layered and glossy as black wax
and our moon blue skin was all
we danced in. Our hearts
were pomegranates. Our hands

were an offering to air. I had never
opened my mouth, until the nightjar
opened its own. Only the monkeys
had male eyes, their little hands bright
with pollen, their tails curled and swaying.

We wrote love across the dust
with the stamp of our bare feet,
until only one sound remained:
the beating heart of the hummingbird
on your brow. But love

we are ghosts of ourselves.
We danced our way out of the garden
and we are lost. Love,
put on your chartreuse dress.
The world has hurt us.
Let us cut off our hair
and remake it.

Stag Boy

Inspired by a painting by Clive Hicks-Jenkins

It's late and the cafe is closed. He comes
in his military uniform, colours cut slant,
not quite from any country you could name.
He fought on the front lines with your brother,
comes with a letter folded and folded again
and the pockets of his jacket are full of coins
and coloured wrappers and half-smoked
cigarettes. He comes with a bag on his shoulder
and it crunches out a noise of bells
when dropped. You feed him soup and whiskey,
stood each side of the cafe counter beneath
a single light. Moths drop at the windows.
In the square outside blossom falls
from the lime tree, and a woman cuts the corner
through a pool of light. He drinks soup
from the bowl, sets out a soft pack
to smoke when he's done, asks for more.
It does not seem to matter when he lies,
or when he tells the truth. He's brought you
flowers, half-dead, some of them straggling roots
as though he tugged them up from some grown-out
verge that morning. Poppies with folded petals,
campions, purple honesty edged with green coin
cases. They'll come back, he says, in water.
That night you lie thinking of him in the cafe below,
kit rolled out behind the bar, sleeping
in his boots under your blankets, lie there thinking
of his dirty hands and the glint of him
through all that, but the stairs don't creak
and no door rattles. Later still, with morning
grey at the city's heels, you watch him
from your window in the scrubland behind the building,
and he's opened up his pack, and the little bells
prick at the dim hour, and he looks regal there
in his brocade, his crown of tangled antlers.

The Fir Church

*In Romanian tradition, shepherds would plant circles of fir trees in hidden places, and hold
secret weddings there when they knew the families of their lovers would not approve.*

Here my father's father found the hand
of his wife, held it above the place
where mushrooms bloom from the earth's tongue.
This tumble of granite and moss was their altar
but they left the fir church belonging
to each other, and the ram's horns
wore ribbons for fully a month, he said.
And we two, shy, proud as roosters
in our embroidered waistcoats, our caps
against the cold. In the fir church words
are not important: only the way the wind
turns aside to let a small fire burn.
Beyond the trees my flock mingles with yours,
the rams' horns decked with moss.

Let love be the smell of lanolin.
Let our promises be unspoken things,
names for the spaces between trees, the gaps
between stones. These silences I offer
in each cupped palm can hold my happiness.

At dawn we wake to embers, crack
the coat of frost across our blanket.
In the night, deer have come in quiet,
gathered in at the wood's fringe, offered
their vulnerability like a blessing.

Travelling Europe with Brienne of Tarth Instead of You

Outside Venice, on a small campsite, we sat
on the shore and ate garlic sausage. She
was too long for the tent, and slept
with her feet in the cool night air;
mosquitos disdained her. I was jealous
of that. Even in the long lines
outside the Basilica she kept her sword
sheathed, only chinking an inch of steel
outside the Cafe Florian, where the surcharge
was quickly lowered. From there,
the train: distant alps, thin young women
bragging their boredom in clouds of smoke.
Genoa announced the nightfall
with gunshots. We ate bad gnocchi,
caught the wrong bus, kissed in the shadow
of a drab billboard before a wooded hill.
The heat came and went like a tide.
By the time the boat reached Barcelona
both of us were pink with too much sun,
oranges and octopus, strong coffee. Everywhere
there were small dogs that eyed us
with reproach. Every surface was ornate.
From the top of the hill, out of breath
with each other, we looked out
over the city, her armour a beacon
of sunlight that drew children and pigeons.
Scaffolding wreathed La Sagrada Familia
like holly. She was careful
that her gauntlet's intricate joints
didn't pinch my hand. The words
we spoke were like leaves blooming
on lime trees. At night we sat side by side
on our balcony above Las Ramblas,
where fruit flies shocked into air
from yesterday's pears, and tourists
spilled like coins across the cobbles.
Everything was in motion, even then.

When we shed our shyness it went easily.
It went like it was meant to. There were tickets
in my bag for the early train to Paris,
where in a Moroccan cafe near the Louvre,
she would set her sword down across the table,
take my hand in hers.

Pilgrimage

The sea slices through me like glass.
Salt-speak crystalises my mouth, so that to utter
each syllable slices my lips. That enormous
sound as the outdrawn wave sucks water
from the pebbled beach. This is my nurse,
Jessie. She tucks my handbag at my feet. My skull
soft with the tide's repetitions, now. Where water
wicks colour from the world, I tilt back my head:
white pebbles, my palm wet, my secrets
swallowed whole. I squeeze her hand
if I need to, if anything hurts. I swallow
the snake. I bite against plastic.
The needle pierces from my primary bronchus
into the heart of the ocean. Water swells.
My levels drop. Shapes move and twist
on the screen above my head. An easy pilgrimage
is no pilgrimage at all. The needle pierces
like glass. Water washes through my lung,
is sucked back up into the tube. That enormous
sound. Jessie, sink into the sea with me.
The snake opens its mouth, the screen buzzes,
the great numbness in my throat is a sponge.
The worst is pulling it out. I speak
the snake; I speak the salt-words, pulled upright,
spilling apologies. The shore is white
with shining instruments. Women in blue
with their backs turned; women in blue weaving
the dunes to the water. The tough grass.
The water receding to its horizon, even
the sun sinking to its calm line, even
the pools where we dropped rocks
smooth now, and empty.

7th Nerve

*Bell's palsy is a neurological condition resulting from damage to the 7th cranial nerve,
and typified by partial facial paralysis and pain on one side of the head.*

Show me your teeth. Can you lift your arms?
Try to smile. Close your eyes. Swallow.
Dive into the dark water. Lie still
while the machine passes around you
and a voice reaches you from another room
where music is playing.
Is it just that side?

Plosives soften to nothing. Language leaks
from the corners of my mouth. All night
my eye tries to see into the dark,
and there is a wave in my ear that breaks
and breaks. Show me

your teeth. Lift your arms.
Snarl like the weasel arcing
towards the rabbit.

Beast in the blinding light. Burnt-tongue.
Fire upon the moors. Show me
your smile, your one bright eye, shed your skin
like a snake. Let that mask melt
off your wrong red mouth.

Come fast through the grass,
some old monster finding
its folklore. Show me
your teeth.

The Leech House

She says he is older than me. I think it is a lie,
but in his tank (round, like a chalice), he moves
like an eel; he moves like a dream. Come winter
someone must stoke the fire in the leech house,
bring fresh moss, sweep out the channel in the floor
where the river sends its emissary, while behind their glass
the leeches dance. My lady has me mark on little labels
when each leech has last been fed: a leech
can live a year without blood, but each dark moon
when the fever comes for her, he lies across her calf,
or sometimes the smooth warm skin at the crook
of her elbow. I scrub his tank clean while he is out of it.
She says a leech is her true companion: the only thing
that knows blood as well as a woman. Is it strange
she has a favourite? Fresh earth for him, and cold clean
water, and green pond moss. I do not like to look
when he is feeding, but she smiles, and it is relief
in her face, not fondness, as if as he drank he took from her
the knowledge of a thing so painful she could not bear
to know it.

Feeding the Five Thousand

Mary Mallon, known as Typhoid Mary, was a cook responsible for the deaths of thousands
of people after knowingly spreading typhoid — or three, depending on who you ask.

That first year the streets were thick
with fog. God went through it like a man
picking eggs from waterglass
and marked sickness on the brows of those
who deserved sickness. And if my hand was his hand
then it was his hand, and what was not good
was not well.

A fever lay on the river and I made peach
ice cream, lobster salad, currant jelly the same
gleaming scarlet as a bleeding heart.
I was god's prayer, I lay on his tongue un-
spoken. Sickness narrows the soul to a point
but my soul

was spreading: even the river could not
contain it. God says that plagues come
as a punishment, but nourishment was my weapon
and I fattened the city
on my wrath.

Drones fly over the Han river in Seoul to encourage wearing a mask

Summer was humid that year,
the river full of apricot stones
washed down from the country.
Two gods above a city
wore masks.

The harbour bared its belly
to light: the skyline bowed
to where the water slicked down
details like a cat licking fur.
Two gods above a city, their mouths

muffled but close, intimate,
silent in the night. Consider
how light travels, arriving always
to darkness. A school of fish
in black water, never still, its million
permutations flexing maths
like a fist. Two gods above a city:
they are staring at each other, silent.

Like starlight
we split ourselves in two.

Outliers

That winter swans came and littered
the fields like torn papers. The air
was always rowdy; water rose until glints
of a strange sky were everywhere

beneath our feet. And then this:
north of Trondheim a black swan flying overhead,
its red bill closed on the star that sat
beneath its tongue.

The thaw followed us north. War
left our souls ruinous. We stood   on street
corners   bearing witness to nameless motions,
  small revolts, snow   falling on a huddled militia
    in the glow of traffic signals and I

    I have an ache in my left eye too
      like the press of a thumb
                    with the twitch
                        of a fly for a pulse –

but we dance soft   in the swallowed mud
      and across the surface of things
              we betray ourselves   in mathematics.

Patterns
        throng the chaos with harmonies,   notes
                that bite their brothers   from the busy air,
                      smoke scudding
                across the   rising   water

      and the weather
            is wrong.

17

Each night stones

        pry   free   of their sockets

             to plumb   the dark's   depth.

   The star

        is under

            my tongue.

Flint, Skomer

The rind of it like milkskin, boiled
under angled eaves of smoke. Light
comes through it like light through the wing
of something rising: when the feathers peel
from one another, and the stretch of bone and sinew
describes all that is good in a morning.

Look: where the stone is broken
there are grooves, small serrations
that mean it was held once and honed
and when a useful whole had been taken from it
dropped. Nearby, jackdaws rouse their rabble
from the bracken, young ones with their eyes still blue.

From here they clear the edge of the island
snagged on the frayed edge of the wind,
tumbled through the air's soft hands.
And on the clifftop, turned always
towards the mainland, where dairy trucks wedge
the narrow lanes, there is a stone.

Upright, tall as a man, the suggestion
of something human in its weight against the sky.
It tells a simple story: we are here, on this island.
We were here.
We were.

You and I are ghosts in the future's forest

It is a gentle, haunted world. Circumstance
has thrown it far into the future,
but there are things in it you and I
would understand: the way silence settles
across a wet morning and the roe deer
raise their heads. Perhaps, also,
a sense of things that need not find
their equilibrium. Our sighs are vapours:
no myth exists to hold us like a heart in aspic.
Again and again the sun sets, swings
under the earth's belly, lifts a worn edge
of cloud come morning. Perhaps we grieve
for language, realising our fluency was false. Words
are a closed loop. A tight knot.
The roe deer raise their heads, move
between the trees, listening for wolves.

Pale moths and the moon's white light.
Where once we walked, water rises.
You and I are ghosts in the future's forest.

Event Horizons

Dear sir, please accept my application
for the position of poet not in residence.
When your robot (which you have named

Grace) passes over the lip of the black hole
I would like to go with her, or at least
to send some poems.

I would like to sit in a dark room
and let the feeds from Grace's cameras
drip ink into my eyes.

I would like to advise your engineers
when they compose her final
poignant tweet. Grace and I have lived

in the same vaulted spaces, where men
examined our component parts and declared
them fit or wanting. We have sat quiet

while others spoke, we have coded
and decoded ourselves, we have performed
well. It is a long way to Monoceros

but the pulse of a binary star is like
a heartbeat. It has to be enough. Grace and I
are linked by a silver thread:

her cameras and spectrometers make her
like a beast, bristling and wary, and we are listening
so carefully, because the dark is never empty.

Grace has thirteen thousand burn sequences
in case of debris; I have brought my notebook
and a snack. There is a knack

to jumping. Grace can calculate her own descent,
a perfect Fibonacci spiral in reverse, but it is wise
to anticipate that she will begin to break: a silver thread,

and a silver needle, and a star orbiting a black hole
6.6 times the mass of the sun. The roar of it. So big
you cannot be close, only catastrophically involved.

Grace, I say, is it beautiful? But the data is good, the data
is what matters. They tell me: an event horizon
is merely a loss of signal. I think: a secret. A silver lock,'

a silver key. Grace, they are cheering.
Are you falling, Grace, are you always falling,
or Grace, did you escape?

Goliat

Not for us the southern siren's song
nor the lamp-eyed blink of the deep sea mermaid,
spined and strung with lights. Not for us
the selkie's seal-skin, easily slipped
on the dawn-slick rocks, nor the tigershark tails
of the tropics' basking women, roped hair knotted
into nets. Not for us these lovely
momentary things, flickered in the shallows
of an epoch. Only

the singular infinities of the wintering sea,
our boomed calls braided
into whalesong, our bodies
mottled like mackerel, measured
in ship lengths,
scarred as old trees.

Not for us the shore. Not for us
its pale sweep like a bone left for the bears to gnaw,
or the long green song of the broken sky. Only the tug
of the north, and the taint of oil, and the urge

to aim ourselves
like arrows in the warming water
and beach.

And the white wood
at the waterline
is like our bodies.

Concerning the Care of Monsters

There are always hounds in the hills.
They mainly run on misty nights, baying
into the dark, setting the chickens to fluster.
On Sundays I leave a plate at the edge
of the wood, scraps of lamb and gravy,
two pale bones. But listen:
close the windows tight. Watch
for the press of fat fingers against the glass,
the hungry look of an infant eye, the long tongue
for tasting lamp oil. Past midnight, take a broom
for shooing, set out the last lamp in the rustling
rhubarb plot, and watch them cluster closer.
They're more afraid of you – you know the rest.
Cerberus knows to wait his turn, three gentle mouths
take chicken breasts, roasted fresh, from my fingers.
He likes to lie in the open door, watching bees
in the pot of pansies, one head turned
towards the pheasant in the field that winds
the year's spring towards autumn. I've heard
that eating fairy food will trap a man
the wrong side of a circle, but I have fed a faun
and since then never could be rid of him:
his little hooves on the flagstones, the way he eyes
the rayburn, asking for pasties, and dim sum,
and the good coffee. Only on moonless nights
do I put on my wellies and take the torch
down into the dingle. Trickling water
echoes among the ferns and the stream shallows out
where sheep kneel in the pebbles to drink.
As mermaids go, she's amiable, has tempted no one
to their doom in ages. We light candles
on the flat rock, eat cold pasta salad, her troutskin tail
shifting in the dark stream. She's good for gossip,
even if she has been banned from the village hall.
Before I go, I brush her hair: One hundred strokes.
Self-care is important, I tell her. I kiss her cheek,
leave her with a magazine, walk back through the churchyard,
where I pat the heads of zombies that sprout

like mushrooms in the damp weather.
From the road the house glows with light,
bleaches the sky to brown, and the black shapes
hunched along the roof raise clawed little hands
and wave.

Lords of the Wasteland

Each piece of good ground the size
of a fat gold coin. Where the willowherb
clogs puddles with its softness
and sleepers stack the numbers of industry
against an untaut acreage of buddleia and diesel,
the floodlit night is feudal with cats.

Here the hemlock is strung with caterpillar silk.
Cold steel like the arc of a tightrope
in the weed-killed gravel. Gravity
is toothless in this fiefdom.
The laws of the land are in the vertical:
the pendulum swing of a tail

arrested mid-jump by the scattered light
from a police car. His majesty
is in his utter indifference; the casual way
he lifts a paw to lick, then holds it,
poised in the cool air while a rat

burrows deeper into shadow. A distant engine;
some stuttered note as the wind moves old metal;
the cold edge of the night. His court,
operatic in their nightly dramas, pace out
the old dances across the yard. They know
how morsels of a living can be found here:

the size of a fat gold coin,
the size of a cat's paw.

Then when you have turned again towards the north

From an artwork by Sharon Hall Shipp

Days when the light was long here
I dashed my shadow out ahead
like a woman throwing water from a bucket.

Thought of the brown cat and the wind
always the wind against the edge of things, and
old cassettes in the gutter spilling their glitter,

and the ivy riddled with sparrows. When
in the winter snow fell on Sun Square in great
slow flakes it whittled the air foreign.

Nothing settled. The long dark shop once filled
with faded VHS hollowed into newness;
slick tile floors and the smell of sulphates.

Behind the library with its colonnades
and damp green sandstone, where you and I
once sat to watch pigeons strut and harass,

the flags are rotten with holes the size
of thumbprints. A bar behind the old Woolworths
slides music into the street like a damp beermat.

The things I pretended still kick
along the pavement: contingencies waiting
to be wanted in the grey light before rain.

Doggerland

The white fronted goose, which migrates to Britain from the arctic over the Dogger bank, was added to the RSPB redlist in 2018

The whole of the earth
is a lens for this longing:
a plucked string snagged
on the wind's hook,
a wing over water,
and the moon's
white urge into winter,
where the rivers seize.

But always
the waters rise.
Always the sea
slackens.

Ice loosens its knots
in the rope of the water
and you

– a knot in the rope
of the air –

unravel:

The shadow of a wing
on the rind of the water
and then nothing.

Dirtwife

One

Goldenrod, mainly flowers. September 88.
Mordant: Alum. Dyestuff: Fresh.
Fleece: Romney. Simmered one and one half hours.

Milk is our mordant. Like bark
we peel back silks to reveal
something that darkens in sunlight.
Time's weft weakens along seams
where memories diverge, paths splitting
between goat willows where water
swells the stones. We delve in the deep earth,
bring pigments to grind, rub our palms together until,
like insects punctuating a summer night,
our bodies become a song.

We give new names to metals long
made meaningless: sort piles of copper pennies,
old nails, flakes of rusted iron from the roof
of the old barn, tin you can snip with scissors.
Lanolin filled winter to its brim, each night
ravelled and plied with its own indigo,
but now a new alchemy takes hold: black
eucalyptus. The closed mouth of the sealed jar.
The smell of things becoming other
in the space beneath the stairs.

Two

Chamomile, whole. August 97.
Mordant: Iron. Dyestuff: Dried.
Fleece: Crossbreed. Simmered one hour.

Time is an intimate thing, reducing objects
to the palm's scale. Come March, when rain
has washed the bare fields clean, the past is naked
to the air. A curve of earthenware, broken
so long that wholeness becomes irrelevant,
unwieldy. Pieces of a past that speaks
of kindness, of milled corn, of pig bones.
Of the earth, when questioned with fire,
answering in two colours: bone yellow, soil
red. And still we tread the clay,
slick to the knees, laughing.

Three

Blackberries. September 83.
Mordant: Iron. Dyestuff: fresh.
Fleece: Shetland. Simmered one and one half hours.

It takes small hands to reach into the hedge. One hundred
tiny buttons down the front of a dress. Somehow,
like a spell, we wake each hour of the night's stretch
to stir the pot; the clockmaker's magic is a beating heart.
Hand over hand through steam we come to the root,
this burnt tongue that turns it all to ink. Our stained
fingers pressing perfection into the hem of a skirt,
so that each year is another inch
before the cloth is turned. Look:

On Salt Pie Lane the sky is blue with flies,
smoke and the stink of urine. The gutters run with colours
complex as oil. It is dyeing day: women have strung
the street with silks of indigo and saffron,
madder and snail shell purple.

Ours is the first chemistry, a science of stone.
This ancient syllabary perpetrates change
upon itself like a ritual, a revelry of reactions
that spreads through fire and salt.

Four

Lavender, dried hearts. October 78.
Mordant: Copper and acetic acid. Dyestuff: dried.
Fleece: Suffolk. Simmered half an hour.

The hill is a thing comprised of apples
and the dark sleep of the barrow. Horses describe
its limits under the settling fog, their tails
an imagined softness, their shapes a half-seen dance
far off in the field, where the ink draws its curtain
across water. But the hill's cheek is turned
towards June, a day when the grass is long

and yellow. The whole of the horizon held
between two colours: the cupped hand's
landscape. We walk out into the open light
where birds are witness to the sinking sun's eye
and things have begun the procession
of their meanings. We remember the tightly tied
knot of winter, how soon, harebells

will toll the sky's blue through everything
and proclaim us past the season's fulcrum. But now
the earth's colours stain us with summer,
leave pollen golden on our eyelids,
mark our palms with umber,
dye us blue and brown.

The Tangible World

We are strangers here.
It's not that we've forgotten
what simple things mean, not
that we do not value the softness
of lambsear or the way light bounds
across wet tarmac at night, more
that they have become slick
to our grip, and we slide across hours
like oiled metal. Time sags
like stretched elastic. There is so much
to be perceived

and so little time left.
We stand so that our shadows
do not mar the picture, wait
until the street is empty. Our feeds
are glorious solitude, an empty world
of architecture and warm light
and flower stalls in summer,
and the sense that this is the world
we have inherited, but we are waiting
for it to happen, standing carefully
out of the sun, taking photographs.
Like god, we codify the tangible world
into proof of our existence:

basil / woodgrain / paper
ocean / mountain / shoe
cactus / poem / window
light / light / light

What was Left in the Orchard

Herefordshire has more acres of orchard than any other county in the UK. They were harvested almost exclusively by workers from the EU.

The trees strung with crow calls
and slack brown fruit. The Wasp Apple.
The Iron Pin. The Ten Commandments. Pomeroy,
and the Green Purnell, and the Cat's Head,
and the Rymer. The Credenhill Pippin, the Onibury Pippin,
the Puckrupp Pippin and the Pig's Nose. A rubble
of apples cobbling the red earth, banked
against the hedges, strewn under the grass
and seeding snowdrops where they rot.
Slowly winter opens the landscape to the eye
of the blackbird, but the harvest
never happened. Apples bred to the size
of a palm fall through empty air
into the wet grass
and rot there.

Hats full, caps full,
bushels and bushels and sacks.

The Ragged Kingdom

November levels the landscape to rubble.
There's smoke in the round houses of the trees
and in the garden, fire opens like a blossom.

Each night water rises all across the fields
and the sodden moon rots to rind, bleaches sickness
into rocks at the water's edge

so that they seem soluble to their own shadows,
granular with time. The tarn's mouth is stopped with ice
but between intersecting fogs are small perfections:

three red berries on the black earth, and a path
between the elders like a dance. And when I turn back
to where my own footsteps darken the frosted field, this:

The tracks of some animal approaching my own, but stopping short,
perhaps watching for a moment, then turning away
and skimming its own path back towards the wood.

Paper Streets

"The rules of the art of 'following' are simple: choose a stranger and secretly copy their route — you'll see the city in a new light" The Guardian, 21 September 2018

The way a penknife cuts through the stem of a fig,
beside the blue doors on the Rue Barbette.

Overhead, the windows sing harmonies to each other,
unafraid of eye contact. I choose your yellow coat

because it is like my yellow coat. I eat the fig
in the rain that is easing into mist, the air

particulate against our skins. Rue des Ecouffe:
three playing cards on the wet pavement, the heel

of your boot leaves a print through the heart;
Jack with the smile, jack with the one eye. We are just

invisible enough. Our intimacies are oblivious.
By the Pont Marie, sycamore leaves break

in the air. It is September: light is yellow
on the water, on the walls of L'ilot Vache, on your hair.

When you turn, I speak into my phone, pantomiming
innocence. I say, *it's me. Yes? I would like —*

You buy a paper. You are checking your change.
You think you are not worthy of notice, but I have seen

your naked decisions, the way you move through the city,
the way your left ankle is braced and your scarf

keeps unlooping from your neck. These are the rules:
if you confront me, I will stop. If you go into a house,

I will stop. I do not wish to alarm you. You see,
I love you, today, the way a thread loves the needle

that pulls it through cloth. You see, I am helpless: victim
to the colour of your hair, the way your yellow coat

beacons against shop windows. We walk together
through the city, each at the end of intersecting rays

of light, and the air between us is a single edifice.
This is my cleverness: I will go into the city, let you

lead me wherever you wish. I will strip back
the emblems of my thought until the streets are bare

of everything but our conspiracy. On the Rue Valette
it is new and perfect; they are digging up the road. Cars

slide against each other in curved reflections
and the world is frictionless even under the sound

of the drills. But you have stopped. You are looking at me;
you lift your phone and take my photograph.

You have been a perfect algorithm. I give you back
your anonymity like a gift. You see: I do not wish

to alarm you. This is my cleverness: I will go
into the city, let you lead me, and then let you go.

St Ives, February

The sea in winter, when light falls like static
upon the drizzled waves. Space still above its plane
for thunder's boom, space for clouds
to sew the seeds of their grandeur, a towering inhalation
from which the water breathes salt. Early morning:
gulls are dropping mussels onto the roof.
Light angles in, levering vermilion
into a palette of greys. Soon
swifts will come on confused winds,
thread the open lines of the town with their calls,
and in their eyes a strange blooming
of early summer flowers.

Full Moon on Fish Street

That year Aubrey's work was characterised by unusual touches of gentle colour among the harsher lines more typical of her style. The series of watercolour sketches she had made between March and September entitled *Tidelines I − XII* are often cited as a turning point in her work, showing as they do a series of local rituals and ceremonies which were becoming all the more common in Cornwall at the time, and which took their inspiration from ancient folk practices with origins in pre-Christian Britain. The first of these, *At the shore in Portreath*, depicts a procession of women festooned with strips of dyed linen making their way across the beach to the shallows. They are sturdy and middle aged for the most part, with reddened faces in the bright sunlight, and rolled up sleeves. The seawater is a beguiling pale jade. On a precarious-looking sedan carried above their heads is a teenage girl, in whose lap a white cockerel sits, tied with twine and ivy. It is a scene with the arrested motion of a photograph: the girl's hair blown up by the wind, the chair itself leaning sharply to one side, the women's feet churning the sea to a cloudy ochre. But the moment we wait for never comes: we are not privy to the ritual performed by these women in the shallows. We never see the cockerel's blood.

What it means to us in winter

In places where the land wagers time
against the tide's unceasing cycle
and thistledown softens the frayed weft
of the wood, night's heraldry is simple:

the yellow moon; the silver fish hidden
in weed; the sea, and what
it means to us in winter.

Sea Change

Something came to shore
and the new moon's thin
light fell askance upon it. Things
in the deep sang the sea's
longing; but it was lost to them
and knew only the way
the windows of the town
shone in darkness;
the cobbles uneven
as it stumbled into the new
moon's darkened streets.

The Unlovely Sea, a third sketch in the *Tidelines* series, can be seen, partially finished, in the background of several photographs, most notably those taken at a party Aubrey threw in the winter of 1924. In these photographs the image is especially clear: a doorway spilling white light onto a whitewashed wall, two pairs of boots, a basket. A sealskin coat hanging from a line of pegs where a straw hat is slowly losing a battle against time and gravity. Through the doorway we can see an offering on the doorstep: a bowl of milk and a bundle of mint. Beyond, there are rows of fish curing in the sun on a birchwood frame. Smoke blows in from an unseen fire, making the distance a bleached expanse of faint, gestural marks which suggest a shoreline, the sea, the edge of a wood.

The left-hand side of the painting is partially obscured in the photograph by the figure of Elizabeth Kidd. Newly arrived in St Ives from Penzance at the beginning of the year, she is standing apart from her brother, and is caught in motion: her long hair a grainy smudge; one thin arm with its articulated elbow; the suggestion of a smile and downcast eyes. The mandolin in her hand catches the light. The artist is next to her in profile. It is impossible to tell where she is looking.

Things that Elizabeth Is

Phosphorescent under the elm.
Rooted into the surface of the world.
Narrow as a cat's eye.

A little dagger, a traveller
an imperfect phrase
something unconsolidated
a silhouette moving mistily
through the present moment
without us.

Elizabeth is on the shore
feet sunk into the sand
and seals are kissing her hands.

Amaryllis

The morning hour when milk-light
softens the fire in flowers;

forced lilies which glow in the cold
morning sunlight, their utter indifference
in the window.

Aubrey, exempted in the lane
drawn in by the flare of them:

startled into love
like a word for something indescribable
which sufficed.

A sense of the world continuing
without us

A storm, and candles burning
in the window: sudden laughter
the china rose among dark leaves
words which hang on water asking,
like music, of their own meaning
although they were spoken
in her own voice. Now
is our festival.

We who have been solitary
rise like birds without anchor,
issue from darkness,
spin song across the whole
of the harbour, while the last bell tolls.

In her 1931 essay *Since Then*, the writer and critic Susan Willet-Banks describes the reception the paintings received on their first showing, at a small exhibition in the Porthmeor Studios:

"There was at the time a sense that Aubrey was showing us, not only our pasts and our presents, but that her work represented some presentiment of our future: that she alone could show us with her deft, spare lines, precisely how it would be in the world from now on."

Later, she writes that, "Aubrey, in her unflinching documentation, casts a foreign light on those rituals which were enjoying a resurgence in the folk consciousness of southern Britain. Even the clouds of dust on the horizon in *Three weeks after the drought* are illuminated in a stark light, the sun a small red eye above, the town of St Ives described in planes of ochre and Payne's grey and pink, and the pyres along the beach flaring a cold, phosphorescent white in contrast. It was as if in our desperation to appease the natural world, we were only setting ourselves further apart from it."

The Heath

She knew this change
but still some quality drew her
into the garden: the slopes running
purple into heather; the distant sky;
the way the breeze played
mellow into the season

and beneath this
wildfire pricking a pale note
of pain into the eye,
the white root of ancient gorse
pressed through the soft palate
of the sky.

Pavane

In summer rooms they cancelled
the silence with a dance:
the creak of floorboards,
thin feet thudding a punctuation,
the blackbird waking into dusk
outside the window. Later
their hands clasped, released.
Even after the sun had set
geraniums turned their cheeks
to the heat of the wall
and loosed their dry scent.

Full Moon, Fish Street

The shore full with night;
a clean still room
and the sea. How
they almost faltered
but were gently, tenderly, falling.

Nothing broke until dawn
somewhere
lifted;
broke the veil.

Lizzie with the gypsies, the seventh painting in the *Tidelines* sequence, shows a meeting on a dusty track through a hay meadow at an unknown location thought to be somewhere near Penzance. Kidd appears in the centre of the canvas, the neck of her mandolin held loosely in one hand "like the neck of a dead goose," her bare, bony feet and her simple white dress stained with dust. Her eyes are closed, and she is singing, an earnest yet unearthly expression of effort on her face, as though she is harnessing with her song some obscure power normally inaccessible.

All around her in the stubble of cut hay there are shadowed figures. They are plainly observing, but it is difficult to make out their expressions; some of the men appear to have removed hats which they are holding almost reverently to their chests. Even the children dotted among them seem to be listening quietly. One, standing closer to Kidd than the rest, is holding a burning torch which casts a dim orange glow. At his feet, a hare with ragged ears is sitting in the dirt.

I know what loves are trembling into fire

We have chosen. All simmered
and shook and after

these things remain: a grey moth's wing
the necessary quiver of our words
your softness, your rough hands

the unprotected fibre
of a flesh which knots itself into air,
the edge of a beech wood where pigeons
break the leaves' light, a town laid out
at the narrow limits of the shore:
everything.

Porthgwidden, November

Your wishes changed, became
for a moment, the coffee-house:
flowers, and a mania of light
as though a star rose
from behind the town. The fire
on the beach already faint,
the sea's roar stronger
than wine. How everything burnt
at the edge of the sea
escapes.

Unlike the other eleven artworks, all of which depict in curious, almost scientific detail a series of strange and human superstitions, the last, *Low tide at Lamorna,* is empty. The only sign of occupation that we are privy to is itself contentious: three darker marks in the sand, which could be footprints already eroded by the waves, are all the clue we have that the beach was ever witness to human occupation.

The beach is a flat greyish yellow, marked by the retreating tide and flanked by steep hills tangled in bramble and ivy. In the tender sunlight the surface of the sea seems a more plastic boundary: a borderland of mist that betrays the eye, and within it are glints of light that showcase the spare mark-making and deftness of colour that Aubrey later became famous for.

Low tide at Lamorna and *The Unlovely Sea* are the only two pieces of Aubrey's work no longer available for viewing by the public. The former resides in a private collection, and *The Unlovely Sea*, with its sealskin coat and humble offerings, was given by Aubrey to Elizabeth Kidd in 1925, and was subsequently not seen again.

What Matters

What matters is the moonlight
on the moor. The way it snags
thistledown on the teeth of a tide
that brushes the year down flat
as cat's fur. What matters

are the skylarks whittling complexity
from a single note that rises
into the dusk. These things
and the journey each spring
that Aubrey makes to the shore.

Rat Boy

Rat boy comes in inching down alleys, bits of straw on him
from a packed barrel. His mask is already on, waxed string tight
to the shorn sides of his head, rat face pushed up
so that his own face seems tender: an exposed throat,
a vulnerability. A mistake. His smile isn't like a rat's at all.

He's been busking down the Narrows, a drum's rhythms dashed
across leather, sunshine and spilled coffee on his black boots
his faded kilt, every pocket heavy with coins, little packets of sugar.
Again the wind rattles down the alleys after him
like the barking of a dog.

It isn't until dark that he pulls the rat's face down over his own,
Stands in the open door with his drum and his tipper, a candle's light
slicked down one shoulder of his jacket. The old lime tree
in the square is rustling with jackdaws hustled from their roost
and across the town the drone of a hurdy gurdy starts up.

That rasp of rough velvet. He bounces the rhythm around town,
kicks it down gutters, rattles it against the doors of the cathedral
and the drone keeps on somewhere behind him but never close.
We look for each other and call to each other but we never meet.
I think that's what he's saying. The drum goes on, further into the night.

Southiou

Khadija Saye has turned her back
towards the camera, the curve of her cheek
luminous as the new moon. Even the flesh
of the photograph is insubstantial, riddled
with hollows the way the bone of the skull
is gauzy beneath a microscope. Khadija Saye
has turned her back towards me.

Think of her in the darkroom, the air
rough with chemicals, the darkness bisected again
and again as she counts out exposures.
The heat and the smell of nitrate. Khadija Saye
has turned her back; silver and tin, the way
light slides against a thing
and makes it simple.

But elsewhere smoke might sink
into the infinite earth:

In a darkened room one of Khadija Saye's photographs
sluices its shadow into a bath of collodion
and she counts backwards,
seven, six, five, until all that is left
is a blank page and the smell of silver in the dark
and the reflection of her face.

At the bottom of a tower a crowd has gathered.
They are throwing gifts into the open arms of the sky.

Driftwood

After Beach Study, Sizewell, by Jane Dowling

That winter my arms
became driftwood
and were washed away.
Still I guard the sluice
of the shore, sand fleas
and the arc of the white sun
and the water's tongue.
Ghosts are in the tide
piled spume pale,
trailing an iridescent run-off
of SPF. Call me boy Cerberus
of the beach. I will be here
and not-here, watching
the arched backs of the boats
relax into the shallows,
where birds wallow
among the ropes, and those
thronging ghosts pile up
against the pierhead, snag
on all the jetties, beach themselves
into sunlight, where they fight
over sandwiches
with the gulls.

How the Oak Tree Survived the Ice Age

Against this only the south could stand.
Ice struck the chime of the water.
The landscape opened
like a fist unclosing to the eye,
and was scoured back to good
clean rock. Winter pressed in
from the north, and it was a dance,
and it was danced into every place
where the sky lowered the hood of its eye,
and forgot the certainties of spring.

In hidden valleys oaks grew
with their backs to the sun. The earth
was an indrawn breath, the ice
three thousand meters deep.
And at the foot of this great
wall of ice, a girl:

I am seven. I have gathered acorns:
large smooth beauties like conkers,
small beads nested in a socket
like a bramble thicket.
I have not yet realised the world
would be better without us.

Everything is Solved in November

By the ash trees, the old van
rusting to its abstract bones.
There is one that forms a doorway
where a rotten limb collapsed
into the long grass, and since then
children have made a game
of edging through into the pressed dirt
beyond. Their names cut in corners. The open
secret. Further into the field, broken bricks,
a small dip like the divot of a spoon,
fenceposts toppled like the monuments
of old regimes, and the bonfire.
Sometime in September it became
aspirational; the height of it heraldic,
the spread, the heart of old sofa and each
raked lawn after the summer storms.
Those leylandii that cast too long
a shadow; pallets piled with the finesse
of a sous-chef plating fish. It's for
the children. Their faces stained
with greasepaint in the dark. They come
with their effigies to kick at the broken brick,
spilling newsprint and straw,
spitting sugar, pantomiming apes
at the edges of the nightfall.
They clart the wheels of their quad bikes,
and their Guys, each wall-eyed and shedding
nylon from a cheap wig, are all women.
Pile the bonfire higher. Everything
that burns will be consumed.

Weathering

The year topples from its zenith. A lone heron
skims the inversion above the alders, a bale of cold air
clapped against its breast. The redness of berries.
The ice in the eye. The long
last urge towards the darkness, and we
rake the coals, burn the brash, kindle a fist
of fire to mark the path between this year
and the next, between something forgotten
and something only hoped for. We draw in
the strings of ourselves, tuck in tight,
fold the edge of a story around the smooth cold stone
that stays with us – the lump in the throat,
the tip of the tongue, the chill of sour windfalls –
until light falls flat against the palms of our hands, uplifted.

Symmetry

The Great Comet of 1106 appeared on 2 February, and was recorded by astronomers in Wales, England, Japan, Korea, China and Continental Europe. It split into many pieces, known variously throughout history as the Great Comet of 1843, Great Comet of 1882, Comet Pereyra, Comet Ikeya–Seki and C/2011 W3 (Lovejoy).

Like an orange in cupped hands, my heart
halved. Ice calved into the racing dark,
spun giddy with constellations like grit
under the tongue of the sun.
On a long enough timescale, ice
behaves like water. The chaos
of things needing one another,
a shining conglomerate, a star
wonderful to behold. Even then
the world was old, a thing worn slick
to the moon's eye. It turned senseless,
breathed its own salt tide, tripped
into war and out like something
blind. I swung like a pendulum,
counted centuries, hurled light
into the backs of the eyes. I burned
myself alive. This is a love poem.
Time makes of me a flock, a beam forking
like the tongue of a snake. I bisect,
peel beauty from its own skin, unkiss
the sharp edge of night. Ice under the tongue
melts like mercury, speaks a silver syllable
to some internal ear, and far below, engines
catch on a spark, ignite, begin to churn
for more. Later, much later, a footprint;
its utter desecration.

Ways for Men to Die in the Fifties

As if the felled ash willed it, clouds drew in
above the hill. David, with his axe propped rakish
on one shoulder; Mary in the back yard
knee deep among chickens. They say an egg laid
on ascension day protects from lightning,
but it was winter, and the storm was a thing
of strange gifts. It swelled the river, left him
silhouetted by the ash stump, axe above his head.
Smelled like a leg of lamb, she said. Later,
when the heat rose like a tide across Ferryside
Tom borrowed the bus fare to the beach. All that summer
they looked for him, up and down the estuary,
prodding banks of seaweed with walking sticks
until the last day: men lined the street to the beach,
took off their hats as his father passed.

The Silent Game

On Thursday afternoon with the sun
in great rhombuses of light
on all the walls, and the corridors
only just empty of echoes, children
are playing the silent game. They call it
a game, but it is boring: hiding quiet
behind desks and cupboards, staying still even
if the sun is in your eyes, even if your friend
is poking you. They call it silent
even though a noise is the thing
they remember later: footsteps in the corridor,
a man's slow footsteps, a sudden fist
against the classroom door before
he moves on. And if it is a game that they play
almost every month, why is their teacher
so serious, why does she hide with them, who
is looking for them, in this game?
Later the boys run out to play
under the bright sun; they are young
and brave and the world
owes them anything, everything.

Three Ships

We go to the shore
to throw back pearls into the ocean: handfuls
from broken strings that I kept

long after their owners
were gone. The cove is clogged with brambles,
auburn bracken that is remembering

how once it was earth, and could be
again. This is our gift to the sea:
the way nacre bends a spectrum of light

into a sphere, does it again and again
until the pearls in my palm feel a part
of my body; as though they bubble

through the skin at the juncture
of head and heart, until there are too many
to hold. Once the sun sets we see them:

three ships spread across the vagabond horizon, each
a blinking light the same pale vermilion as mars.
They are bringing gifts; they bring nothing;

they come only to observe:
the darkening shore, two girls, the sea
rearing like a horse, and the strangeness

of pearls in the dusklight, lit
and then vanishing easily into the unquiet sea
where they are swallowed and swallowed and swallowed.

Wheatfield with Crows

After Van Gogh

Black crows tossing their silhouettes
against the gold; the never-stillness
of the earth. Remember:

the only time I cried that summer
was after the first all clear
and halfway home from the hospital
we stopped in a valley corked
with apples and silence, and the light

was apricot warm. I stood
at the edge of the field
watched its little tides
thought of the golden haired
women in pre-raphaelite paintings

thought, god, I'm free, thought
how all this would carry on
a little longer, thought of bread
warm from the oven, thought of
cornfields, and the joy of them,
and laughed, and wept,
and watched the black crows
against the gold.

Dung Beetle Love Poem

We hinge our whole hearts
around the pinpoint of a star,
begin the dance: we two
beneath a path of light, the sight of it
written deeper than blood.
Let the sands move around us,
let the moon rise and set in perfect
rhythmic irrelevance. We two are royal
to the future, gleaming like gold
and following a star across the sands.
More precious now than frankincense
is our gift to you: we bring dung, fragrant
as resin, rolled round and perfect.
Beneath a throng of light we bury it
offer it to the sand, which is the future.
This fleeting night: our elegant rhythms,
the heady spinning dark. We know
the dance of spheres from long ago.
What else could love be? To trust
that things will continue, that white light
will fall still upon the sands;
upon you, our children.

Horse Skull Crown

Put on your armour.
It is the autumn of the world
and things are waiting
to be unmade. Put on your armour
of ratskin and finchbone and ash.

Put on your horse skull crown and let
us dance my love. Things glitter
and the night is a tower above us,
so put on your armour
of dead oak and antler and clay.

It is the evening of the world
and meaning unpicks
from words which have died
on our tongues. Put on your armour
of paper and bracken and glass.

Endings buzz in the bones: put on
your horse skull crown. Let's dance
the old dances. Let's speak the old
words. Let us dance in our armour
of plastic and hemlock and oil.

Blackberries

I bring you blackberries.
I give you sweetness in a sour world.
I give you the sun on your back and a cold morning.

I bring you gifts from the edge of the season.
I give you the blackbird's song. I give you
the wasp's drowsy hum. I give you smoke and sugar.

I give you thorns and the old horse stamping.
I give you the russet hill and the hoar frost.
I give you the oak tree's first bronze leaf.

I show you the hill at midnight.
I bring you my heart under the starlit sky.
I open my hand. I give you blackberries.

Acknowledgements

Heartfelt thanks go out to Emma van Woerkom, who was the first to see Goliat as a fledgeling and encouraged it into the world; Jenny, who supported me so generously through a difficult time; Aloki who inspires me every day from across the sea; and my mum, who read to me when I couldn't, and even did the voices.

A note on *Full Moon on Fish Street*: The poems in this sequence are, for the most part, blackout poems which use as their source material words from a single page each of *The Waves* or *To The Lighthouse* by Virginia Woolf. Some of the titles are taken from those works in the form of complete phrases.